Help Me Help You

Maximize The Results Of Your Counseling

Christian Concepts
Centerville, Ohio

Help Me Help You

Published in the United States of America by Christian Concepts (christianconcepts.com), an imprint of New Reflections Counseling, Inc. (newreflectionscounseling.com).

Although the author is a professional counselor, this book is not intended to be a replacement for professional counseling.

First Edition: September 2021

Pavlik, Matthew Edward, 1971-
Help Me Help You / Matt Pavlik.

ISBN: 978-1-951866-06-8 (softcover)

BISAC

1. PSY010000   PSYCHOLOGY / Psychotherapy / Counseling
2. REL050000   RELIGION / Christian Ministry / Counseling & Recovery

Library of Congress

1. Counselor and client
2. Counseling psychology

Related Subjects

Goals, Growth, Self-help, Transference, Counter-transference, Communication, Trust, Therapy, Treatment Plan, Conflict Resolution, Truth, Grace

IMAGES

Cover: https://unsplash.com/photos/w46tRF64qNc
Introduction: pexels - 7902913
Chapter 1: Goal worksheet on page 8 created by Matt Pavlik
Chapter 2: pexels - 3773655
Chapter 3: pixabay - 1972423
Chapter 4:
Chapter 5:
Chapter 6: pixabay - 1867093; pexels - 1640406
Chapter 7:
Chapter 8:
Chapter 9:
Chapter 10:
Chapter 11:
Chapter 12:
Afterword:

CONTENTS

Introduction

How To Be Successful

Have you ever found yourself in dire need of help, but resisted or even rejected the help offered? Asking for help is hard especially when you believe any of the following:
  - The help won't help me.
  - My brokenness is beyond repair.
  - The cure will be worse than the disease.

What do these have in common? They all stir up hopelessness. Why bother if you'll be no better or even worse off for trying?

God's cure is always better than the disease, but to tread on the path to healing requires facing the fullness of your brokenness. You must feel the pain caused by the brokenness of this world.

Help Me Help You is a plea to embrace humility on your quest for a better life. The person who surrenders to God is wise. It is good to trust yourself to God because He is clearly on your side. He rewards those who put their faith in Him (Hebrews 12:6).

Laying your life down in tender surrender before the Lord will bring life, prosperity, and honor as your reward.
—Proverbs 22:4 TPT

To make the connection between surrender, humility, and fear, read a different translation of the same verse.

The reward for humility and fear of the LORD is riches and honor and life.
—Proverbs 22:4 ESV

Those who fear God will surrender to Him. Healthy fear is really acceptance of God's status as Creator and your status as created. It leads to an overall peaceful feeling. Unhealthy fear results from a resistance of this foundational truth. Can anyone challenge their Creator without generating intense anxiety?

*Israel, you have no right
to argue with your Creator.
You are merely a clay pot
shaped by a potter.
The clay doesn't ask,
"Why did you make me this way?
Where are the handles?"*
—Isaiah 45:9 CEV

Do you understand the significance of the help God is offering to you? Whenever you are surrendered to God you have no reason to fear. Think of a time when you were consumed

Help Me Help You

by fear. Now imagine how surrendering to God would have transformed your fear into restful peace.

How I Can Help

I am a professional counselor. I enjoy seeing my clients reach their goals. If I was your counselor, I'd want you to be able to gain the most from your counseling. Being a counselee is a skill you can improve.

Since counseling is highly personal and private many people don't have a realistic model of how the counseling relationship works. TV shows or movies are not the best examples! It pains me that some people would rather get their tooth drilled than to seek healing for their soul. You don't have to be afraid of counseling.

This book is an inside peak into the world of professional counseling. It will increase your confidence in your ability to improve your spiritual, emotional, and mental health through a counseling relationship.

Counseling is highly customizable to your specific needs. It's more than appropriate for clients to ask questions and receive answers that enable this customization process.

You're going to learn some practical information about how to make the most of your counseling experience. *Help Me Help You* has twelve principles (one per chapter) grouped into three parts:
1. Setting and achieving your goals (chapters 1-4)
2. Developing a disciplined inner life (chapters 5-8)
3. Building a healthy relationship with your counselor (chapters 9-12)

Chapter 1

Identify and Pursue Your Goals

What do you hope to gain from counseling? One possible outcome is to achieve an emotional health goal that you can't reach as quickly as you want, or at all, without help. Counseling can breathe new life into your efforts to heal.

Goals Help You Make Progress

Keeping your goals in the forefront of your mind will make your counseling experience more positive and efficient. Measurable goals help you know how close you are to where you want to be. Goals pave the way for results. Knowing where you're going and seeing your progress can be highly motivating.

Consider creating both long-range and short-range goals. A long-range goal is what you want to accomplish by the end of therapy. A short-range goal (also called an objective or step) is what you want to accomplish in the next counseling session. If you string together enough met objectives, you will reach your overall goal.

Goals can be high-level and relational, detailed and specific, or some combination of both. Your goal can be clinical and symptom-focused such as, *I want to stop having panic attacks*. Or, it could be relational and broad such as, *I want to better understand who I am*. Broad goals usually need to be broken down into smaller steps, but they are a great place to start.

SMART Goals
Optimize Your Counseling

Craft your goals so that they are: Specific (are in sufficient detail to be actionable), Measurable (can determine your progress), Achievable (are realistic), Relevant (are important to you), and Time-bound (have a deadline). Here are some examples of S.M.A.R.T. goals:
- I want to lose 10 pounds in 10 weeks.
- I want to decrease my level of anxiety from a 9/10 down to a 3/10 over the next 6 months.
- I want to increase my level of self-esteem from a 1/10 up to a 7/10 in 10 months.
- I want to be able to list 5 of my distinct, defining attributes within 3 months.
- I want to be free from my addiction to food in 7 months.

Identify Your Goals

At the start of your counseling, what would you write down for the following questions?

1. What led to your decision to seek counseling at this time? Why now?
2. What are your goals for counseling (be brief, but as specific as possible)?
3. What do you want to be different about you by the time you finish counseling?

Take your goals outside of your head. Make them concrete by using the Goal Setting form (on the following page) to capture your long-range S.M.A.R.T. goals. To transform your goals (desired reality) into an actionable plan, fill in all five parts of the form.

- (A) Current Reality: Describe up to five undesirable aspects of your current situation.
- (B) Desired Reality: Describe up to five aspects of your goal.
- (C) Obstacles: Describe up to five things (people, limitations, circumstances) that make it harder to reach your goal.
- (D) Resources: Describe up to five things that will help you overcome your obstacles.
- (E) Actions: Describe up to five next steps you can take to move you toward your finish line.

Take Action Toward Your Goals

Writing out your goals will help, but this isn't the number one thing to do in order to reach your goals. If you don't ever start working on your goals, then after five years, you'll be no closer to reaching them. But if you start today, and continue every

(A) CURRENT REALITY

1.

2.

3.

4.

5.

(C) OBSTACLES

1.

2.

3.

4.

5.

(D) RESOURCES

1.

2.

3.

4.

5.

Help Me Help You

(B) DESIRED REALITY

1.

2.

3.

4.

5.

(E) ACTIONS

1.

2.

3.

4.

5.

day, you can see significant results in months. And if that's true, imagine what you'll have accomplished in several years!

*The number #1 way to achieve your goals
is to take action on them every day.*

Attending counseling is one way to take action on your goals. Share your goals with your counselor. When you communicate your goals, you counselor can help you develop and stay focused on a treatment plan—the details for your counseling that indicate how you will achieve your goals.

Monitor your progress and update your goals as often as necessary to stay focused. Review and revise your goals every one to three months. If you've defined your goals, congratulations! Some would say you're halfway to the finish line. Now, make a commitment to work on your goals consistently until you reach them.

When you accomplish one goal, you'll have an idea of the effort required. Then, the counseling process will no longer seem so intimidating or mysterious.

Chapter 2

Seek An Emotionally Significant Experience

Counseling can be informational, relational, and experiential. All three are helpful.

Knowing the rules of soccer (information) is quite different than playing soccer (experiential). Reading about someone who has cancer is one thing (information). Receiving care from another person while you are going through chemotherapy is another (relational).

All else equal, the more you invest emotionally in counseling, the greater the risk and the reward. Consider a swimming analogy. Reading about how to swim is low-risk but it is also low-reward. To really build your skills and grow, getting in the water is necessary. But how deep are you prepared to go? Dipping your toe in the water is a cautious approach. Diving in where the water is above your head is a bold or perhaps careless approach.

What optimal depth do you need to reach so that you can overcome your life problems? Most of the time, the more severe your problem, the more intensive your counseling will need to be to achieve your goals. Therapy can build your resilience against life's struggles and increase your ability to reach your potential.

Informational Therapy

If you seek only information, you'll know more about your problems, but you run the risk of not putting into practice what you are learning. Information can lead to transformation when you experience it relationally. The purpose of counseling is to achieve accelerated growth you can't accomplish on your own.

If you're not sure what to expect from counseling, you might enter into it with caution. The more cautious you are, the more closed you'll be to the counseling experience. This approach might become a self-fulling prophecy that counseling doesn't work.

Receiving information from someone is much less personal than allowing the experience to transform your belief system. For counseling to be personal, you must trust your counselor. The healthiest form of trust builds over time. (A later chapter will cover practical ways to build trust in therapy.)

Relational and Experiential Therapy

Most problems come from a combination of emotional wounds and a lack of spiritual vitality. People become hurt in the context of a relationship, so becoming whole again must also occur in the context of a relationship.

Entering more fully into the counseling process creates an immersive experience—a richer learning environment well beyond what information alone can accomplish. The more immersive counseling becomes, the more it can recreate your life problems. The more you are in touch with your life, the better opportunity you have to resolve your problems.

Usually, more intensity means more transformation—more dramatic and lasting results. Applying a specific truth to your life takes time. More time is needed to build a relationship than it takes to teach information. You can increase the intensity by attending more frequently and being more transparent with what you are thinking, what you are feeling, what you have done, and what you want to do.

To gain more from counseling requires more risk. If you lean toward being risk-averse, that's okay. You can still maximize your results by pushing yourself to the highest risk level you can comfortably tolerate.

I've been a counselor for over twenty years and I've also attended my own counseling for what adds up to over ten years. Here's what I've found. God transforms people more often by bringing them through emotional difficulties than providing a touch of instant healing. If you are in pain and feel scared, but still trust God to help you, you are in good company with the rest of His children.

Chapter 3

Meet Frequently Enough
To Build Momentum

How often should you attend counseling? It depends. How quickly do you want results? Do you want to realize progress in months or years? The faster you want to see results, the more frequently you should meet and the more work you'll need to do in-between sessions.

Two different clients could attend counseling for the same length of time, but one attends weekly and the other attends monthly. The weekly client receives four times the hours and therefore, a more immersive experience.

Meet frequently enough to meet your goals, which includes both time you need and time your counselor needs. You might only want to meet 1x/month but that isn't usually enough for your counselor to get to know you and help.

Low-Commitment Therapy

Solution-focused brief therapy is a valid form of counseling, but it's not for everyone. Solutions are more about fixing than they are about relating. Brief therapy tends to yield more head knowledge because it limits your exposure to the counseling experience.

You might decide you'll only attend six sessions. Or, you might decide to only attend a monthly appointment. While these restrictions might appear to conserve your resources (time and money), instead, they will put an upper limit on the results of your counseling. If your first priority is to reduce cost, you might be better off reading a book.

A danger of attending too infrequently is a lack of momentum. You might become disengaged, put too little effort into the counseling, miss timely feedback on your concerns, and conclude counseling does not work.

High-Commitment Therapy

The more frequently you attend counseling, the more intensive your experience. Usually, more intensity means more dramatic and lasting results.

Let's compare counseling to cooking. Water has a boiling point at which it starts to change from a liquid to a gas. The heat and movement of the water help to cook and tenderize food.

Boiling is an explosive phase change between a liquid state and a gas state. It is used to enhance the texture of starchy foods and tougher proteins, making them more edible. It also revives grains, dried pasta, and dried

Help Me Help You

legumes, making them soft and tender.
—https://www.jessicagavin.com/boiling on July 13, 2021

To boil water you need to supply sufficient heat to cause the water to reach 212 degrees Fahrenheit. Boiling water has the dynamic energy needed to cook the food.

A high emotional temperature in the counseling process is the point at which you become clearly aware of your feelings and are willing to do whatever it takes to resolve the pain in a healthy way. God considers difficult trials as opportunities for growth (James 1:2-4).

A danger of attending too frequently is a lack of time in between sessions during which you can make adjustments and try new behaviors. If you feel too overwhelmed, you might refuse to do any work. You might show up to your next counseling session with nothing new to report, and conclude that you don't need counseling.

When feasible, meet with your counselor weekly or every other week and continue at that pace until you build enough momentum to address your concerns. If you're in crisis, consider 2x/week or 2-hour sessions.

How committed are you to reaching your goals? Count the cost. A saved marriage is less costly than a divorce. Are you ready to invest whatever it takes (time, money, effort) to reach your goals? Investments don't usually pay off immediately. Consider what you will receive if you invest and what you will miss out on if you don't.

Chapter 4

Fulfill Your Role
as a Proactive Participant

To reach your goals, it will be helpful to understand your role and your counselor's role. Fruitful therapy is a life-transforming experience that enables you to meet the challenges of life. It is a cooperative effort between you and your counselor.

Understand Your Counselor's Role

Counseling is more like a gym membership than a doctor visit. A fitness trainer can suggest exercises to promote physical fitness, but their physical activity doesn't cause anyone else to lose weight. In contrast, if a patient has cancer, the doctor operates while the patient does nothing but give permission. Your counselor can point you in the right direction and make suggestions, but you must do the heavy lifting if you want to grow more emotionally healthy.

Counseling is both easy and hard. It's relatively easy to know what you need to do to improve. If you don't think that is obvious, a good first goal is to make a clear treatment plan. Making the necessary changes by putting the ideas into practice is considerably more challenging work.

Your counselor equips, encourages, and empowers. Your counselor can lovingly point you to the truth and suggest a course of action. Your counselor can model God's compassion and care. Insight-oriented questions can help you to better know yourself, feel positive about yourself, and develop your own solutions.

However, your counselor can't "fix" you. Counseling is more of a process you and your counselor go through rather than a "magic pill" which gives instantaneous results with minimal effort.

Understand Your Role

Have you ever heard, "You can lead a horse to water but you can't make it drink"? Sometimes life puts salt in your oats and your thirst drives you into counseling.

You will get out of counseling what you put into it. Your primary responsibility is to be active, not passive. Make a good-faith effort at personal growth and engage in the counseling process as an important priority in your life.

The best counseling is a dynamic process of learning how best to work together to help you create a customized solution to your concerns. Your counselor knows principles of being mentally, emotionally, and spiritual healthy. You decide together how to best apply them to your life. You decide how much you'll act upon what you're learning. To become empowered, you must willingly work to internalize what you're learning and experiencing.

How to Be Active

Try to incorporate as many of these suggestions as you can into each of your counseling sessions.

- Share what's new in your life that's related to the reason you're in counseling.
- Share your agenda and your desired focus.
- Ask questions related to your struggles. This activates your ability to receive what you need most.
- Respond to your counselor's ideas. Share what is working or what doesn't seem to be working.
- Take notes during your session.
- Plan time immediately after your session to assimilate all that you gained. You just took 50 minutes to reach a conclusion. Be sure to capture insights you don't want to forget so you can explore them later.
- Don't wait until the end of your session to ask what you should do or open a whole new topic.

Customize Your Counseling

What kind of experience are you looking for? You might be someone who prefers or needs your counselor to listen. Or, you might benefit from more direct questioning. Participate in your therapy by providing consistent feedback to your counselor. Your counselor can't read your mind, so tell your counselor how you're feeling and what you need.

Following is a list of possible interventions you can ask for in your counseling:

- Listening: you will do more of the talking while your counselor hears and accepts you.
- Empathy: your counselor shares what he understands to be your emotional experience.

- Silence: allows you to collect your thoughts and feel your emotions.
- Scripture: read, reference, and/or discuss Bible verses.
- Prayer: your counselor will pray for your healing as God leads.
- Lament: you will have space so you can share your pain directly to God.
- Assignments: therapeutic work for you to do in-between your sessions.
- Teaching: your counselor will educate you on how counseling works to help you reach your goals.
- Questions: your counselor will ask open-ended questions to help you explore your inner world.
- Direction: your counselor will suggest a course of action based on your goals and circumstances.
- Feedback: your counselor will share insights he has about you as frequently as he notices them.
- Encouragement: as your counselor becomes aware of your positive attributes, he will share them with you.
- Bibliotherapy: your counselor will suggest books to read so you can talk about what you learned.
- Movies: your counselor will suggest movies to watch so you can talk about what you learned.
- Journaling: your counselor will suggest topics to consider as a focus so you can share what you learned or directly share what you wrote.

Chapter 5

Engage Your Heart
with Truth and Grace

Chapters 5 through 9 explore how an internal focus will help you reach your goals.

"Intra" means within, so "Intra-Active" means to be active within. To improve the results of your counseling, it will be helpful to grow in self-awareness and self-understanding. You can start by simply being more reflective and contemplative.

Life-changing therapy enhances the work of God in your life through emotional healing. God wants to help you transform negative beliefs into positives and strengthen you where you are gifted. The best way to accomplish this is to focus on the concerns of your heart.

Internal Growth
Produces External Change

Changing your behavior without changing your attitude produces only temporary change at best. If you really want to grow and keep your changes, first learn the motivations of your heart—the place where the Holy Spirit does His transforming work. Jesus teaches that wrong behavior starts in your heart.

But what comes out of the mouth proceeds from the heart, and this defiles a person. For out of the heart come evil thoughts, murder, adultery, sexual immorality, theft, false witness, slander.
—Matthew 15:18–19 ESV

Jesus brings healing to you from the inside, out. The source of your problems is your heart. What is in your heart produces your thoughts, which in turn influences your feelings and directs your behavior. For therapy to help you long-term, you must expose what is in your heart. While this is hard to do, it produces real results. After you address whatever is troublesome in your heart, your behaviors will improve.

Truth and Grace
Stimulate Internal Growth

Think about a room in your home that is a dirt, dust, and germ magnet. What would happen if you never felt uncomfortable about its condition? It would only become more disgusting. Conversely, what if you believed it could never be clean enough? You might waste time obsessively scrubbing it, wearing out both you and the room's surfaces.

Help Me Help You

When you're not making the progress in counseling you want, it's usually because of one of two reasons. Either you're in too much pain and you need more grace, or, you're not in enough pain and you need more truth. Pain can make your life better or worse, depending upon how you use it. Pain used the right way motivates you to pursue healthy growth.

If you're feeling too raw or vulnerable, you need grace first. The grace you need is encouragement, the softer side of truth. Pain's only purpose is to drive you to make necessary corrections. Pain is always a means to an end, not an end in itself. If your conscience is over-active, then to heal you first need to feel safe and secure. You need a foundation of God's acceptance.

If you're too rebellious or indifferent, you need truth first. The truth you need is conviction, the tougher side of grace. Truth makes you aware of the danger along your path. Truth is graceful because it can save you from your dangerous condition. Truth can be natural consequences from boundaries that prevent further destruction. You need to be in enough pain to motivate you to seek God's help to correct the places of brokenness.

For godly grief produces a repentance
that leads to salvation without regret,
whereas worldly grief produces death.
—2 Corinthians 7:10 ESV

The goal of therapy shouldn't be to numb your pain. Unaddressed pain or no pain when there should be pain, leads to sickness or destruction. A person becomes addicted when they choose a strategy, such as perpetually avoiding pain, that never produces health or growth.

When you begin to look at your pain, you will probably feel worse before you feel better. Short-cuts to health don't exist. Any real, lasting progress requires hard work. Think about a lesson you learned through your own sweat and tears. You don't forget those lessons.

Chapter 6

Focus on Yourself

The purpose of counseling is to help you reach your potential. Because God wants this for you, no other person can prevent your success.

Stop Putting Your Hope In Others' Ability To Change

You can't improve yourself if you're focused on someone else. The person who puts their hope in others' ability to change becomes a slave to them. Your life will be on hold until they decide to change.

Anxiety results when you attempt to control something that is out of your control. When you focus on attempting to change someone else, you'll probably end up frustrated with little, if any, progress.

Criticizing others' performance is an attempt to gain control of your circumstances. It will fail if you haven't first challenged yourself. You'll be too harsh with others and too easy on yourself. Jesus instructs us to stay focused on our issues.

"Judge not, that you be not judged. For with the judgment you pronounce you will be judged, and with the measure you use it will be measured to you. Why do you see the speck that is in your brother's eye, but do not notice the log that is in your own eye? Or how can you say to your brother, 'Let me take the speck out of your eye,' when there is the log in your own eye? You hypocrite, first take the log out of your own eye, and then you will see clearly to take the speck out of your brother's eye.

—Matthew 7:1–5 ESV

Help Me Help You

Focusing on others too much avoids the work and results of therapy. If you spend your precious minutes in your counseling session talking about how much you wish others would change, you're missing out on the power of change. Others might refuse to change, but you have the ability to be satisfied with the changes you can make.

Focus on What You Need

Focusing on yourself requires intentional effort, but it leads to freedom and contentment. Trying to change others usually results in frustration because you don't have the power to do it. It's beyond your control. As you grow, you become less dependent on life happening a certain way in order for you to be happy.

"Ask and it will be given to you; seek and you will find; knock and the door will be opened to you. For everyone who asks receives; the one who seeks finds; and to the one who knocks, the door will be opened.
—Matthew 7:7-8 NIV

You're in counseling to focus specifically on you. Don't feel selfish about the attention; instead, learn how to drink it in. Be willing to be known. Discover and disclose what needs healing. Don't be afraid to ask for what you need. Put into words your longings and your pain.

Focus on What You Can Control

When you stop trying to change others, you accept the world as it is. This saves you energy that you can devote to your own growth.

Worrying is also a waste of energy. It doesn't improve your situation, but it can worsen your situation. When you worry, you are discharging emotional power that could be put to better use. How would your life be different if you could live according to the Serenity Prayer?

> *God, grant me the serenity to accept the things I cannot change, the courage to change the things I can, and the wisdom to know the difference.*
>
> *Living one day at a time, enjoying one moment at a time; accepting hardship as a pathway to peace; taking, as Jesus did, this sinful world as it is, not as I would have it; trusting that You will make all things right if I surrender to Your will; so that I may be reasonably happy in this life and supremely happy with You forever in the next.*
>
> *Amen.*
>
> —Reinhold Niebuhr

By focusing on yourself, you become empowered to live with more peace and confidence.

Chapter 7

Know Your Compelling Reason To Change

How fruitful are your attempts at making changes? To achieve deep, lasting change you often must hit bottom so you feel desperate enough to submit to God's care for you. Repentance is the willingness to move internal obstacles out of the way so God can work in your life. If you ask, God will even help you become more willing to repent.

Lasting change requires ongoing, intentional effort. In other words, it's hard work. Use the following to assess your readiness for change. The Stages of Change model, introduced in the late 1970s by researchers James Prochaska and Carlo DiClemente, proposes six levels of readiness to change:

1. Precontemplation: resisting change. *I've snacked on chips for years, and I've no reason or desire to change now.*

2. Contemplation: identifying your compelling reason to change. *Eating fruit instead of chips would provide more energy to play with my kids.*
3. Preparation: allowing the possibility of change. *I increased my food budget and purchased a bag of apples.*
4. Action: making a change—doing something different. *I ate an apple during my break.*
5. Maintenance: keeping the changes in effect. *I eat an apple every day during my break.*
6. Recycling: reworking preparation and action after relapse. *I realize I'm tired of eating apples every day, so I'll try bananas.*

Where would you say you're at in your readiness for change?

To create successful change, use these three steps:
1. Cultivate your desire to change.
2. Improve your ability to change.
3. Remove your resistances to change.

Cultivate Your Desire to Change

You probably won't change your beliefs, habits, or behaviors unless you're motivated to do so. You won't change, even if change is for the better, unless you are passionately motivated by your compelling reason.

You must know why you want your life to be different.

As long as the perceived rewards of staying as you are remain greater than the rewards of changing, you'll likely stay as you are. As long as the perceived risks of changing are greater than the risks for staying the same, you'll be unlikely to change.

What is your compelling reason? Revisit your goals and make sure they fit with your compelling reason.

Improve Your Ability to Change

Even if the motivation for change exists, you might still need some assistance in changing. If you ignore the dynamics of human behavior, you'll assume that once you understand the need for change, you'll miraculously move in that direction.

What holds you back is your past experiences, ingrained beliefs, uncomfortable feelings and self-deceptive behaviors. You may want to become an assertive person but all your previous living has conditioned you to be passive or aggressive.

The deepest change occurs in the context of a helpful, safe relationship. Relating to another person changes the structure of your brain like no other experience. To change your beliefs and ultimately your behaviors significantly, take full advantage of the help a counseling relationship provides.

In what ways do you need help in making changes?

Remove Your Resistance to Change

Finally, there is the issue of the impact of your changes on others. Consider the impact of your changes on the rest of your family, community, or even society. Expect that others will sometimes resist even positive changes (when they perceive the change will require more effort for them). In making changes, there may be some negotiation involved in determining what is best overall.

Going through with changes, if for the right reasons, is best in the long run. If you believe what you're doing is right, then perseverance is necessary because others will resist your plans. A counselor who is on your side can support you as you work through your resistances. Tell yourself, "It is ok for me to make these changes. I will be improving my health. I am worth it."

Have you given yourself permission to change? What, if any, resistance are you expecting? Are you committed to changing even when faced with resistance?

Chapter 8

Assimilate What You Are Learning

The effectiveness of counseling depends on more than what happens *during* a session. If you want to make the most of your counseling, develop an intentional in-between-session routine that includes these three steps:
1. Reflect: digest your counseling session.
2. Act: practice what you're learning.
3. Plan: prepare for the next session.

Keep your goal in mind as you work through these steps. Try to maximize the number of activities that contribute to your goal. Clear time in your schedule for at least one hour every week for session-boosting activities.

Reflect

Try to capture what you gained immediately after your session. Then, a little later, revisit the experience to identify

what else you gained. The following questions will help you glean what you learned from your counseling session.
- What happened during my session?
- What insights did I gain?
- What questions do I have?
- What helped me improve?
- What blocked my progress?

Organize your answers using the following three prompts:
1. Insights: What I learned from the session on (__/__/____).
2. Assignments: what my counselor suggested I work on.
3. Action Plan: what I plan to do with what I have learned.

Act

When you practice what you are learning, try to keep a balance between internal and external efforts. Internal skills focus on using what is going on inside of you to help you reach your goals. External skills focus on using what is going on outside of you to help you reach your goals. Following are four suggested skills to get you started (but you or your counselor may have others).

Pray (internal)

Ask God to help you make the truths you're learning be real in your life. Ask God to give you further insight into what your counseling revealed.

For this reason, since the day we heard about you, we have not stopped praying for you. We continually ask God to fill you with the knowledge of his will through all the wisdom and understanding that the Spirit gives, so that you may live a life worthy of the Lord and please him in every way: bearing fruit in every good work, growing

in the knowledge of God, being strengthened with all power according to his glorious might so that you may have great endurance and patience, and giving joyful thanks to the Father, who has qualified you to share in the inheritance of his holy people in the kingdom of light.
—Colossians 1:9–12 NIV

Journal (internal)

Be curious about yourself. Notice your feelings and thoughts. Journal about what you're learning in counseling, about your life experience, and about future hopes. Journaling accelerates your progress because it forces you to encounter your experiences from a more objective, outside perspective. Consider using the journal-in-layers method described in *Soar Like Eagles* (see the final pages of this book for details).

Connect (external)

Build relationships with others. Share your insights, your struggles, and your dreams with at least one other person. Learn how others can meet your needs, and how you can contribute to others. You can be healthy, independent, and have emotional needs.

Experiment (external)

If you take piano lessons, your instructor will expect you to practice in-between lessons. When you learn something new in session, you need to experiment with it outside of your session. If your counselor assigned you any homework, put in the effort to complete it. Then consider how the assignment moved you closer to your goal.

When you practice living a new way for long enough, it will become a normal part of your life. Be prepared to share with your counselor the results of your practice.

Plan

Create an agenda for your upcoming session. Include items like questions, insights, hurts, and feedback. Prioritize what you want to focus on. Create a list of questions you have for your counselor. Come prepared to ask for what you want from counseling as well as being open to feedback and suggestions from your counselor.

Organize your answers using the following three prompts:
1. Results: what I learned from what I did.
2. Goal: what I want to work on during my next session on (___/___/_____).
3. Agenda: how I want to accomplish my goal during my next session.

Chapter 9

Share Your Feedback

Chapters 9 through 12 focus on developing a healthy relationship with your counselor.

"Inter" means between, so "Inter-active" means to seek to build the relationship between you and your counselor. Learning how to communication with your counselor will help you make the most of the time you're in counseling. When you feel positive about your counseling, you'll feel free to:

- Be expressive.
- Be responsive.
- Be honest.
- Be collaborative.
- Be transparent.
- Be vulnerable.

Becoming skilled in (or at least familiar with) the following three ways you can give feedback will improve your communication:

1. Process Versus Content

2. Meta-Communication
3. Immediacy

These skills will help you reach your counseling goals quicker and they will also work in your relationships outside of counseling.

Process Versus Content

The *topic* you choose to talk about during your counseling session is its *content*. *How* a counseling session takes place is its *process*. By focusing on the counseling process more than its content, you dramatically improve the opportunity for significant results.

Provide feedback about what is working for you and what isn't working. Feedback allows your counselor to know how well his interventions are helping. Part of counseling is working toward agreement on how best to treat your mental and emotional concerns.

Feedback is different than resolving conflict. Conflict resolution is only needed when there is disagreement about how to proceed. Feedback helps counseling move forward so you can reach your goals. It's not something you only do when you're ready to terminate counseling.

Here are some examples of how you might provide feedback to your counselor:

- Our sessions seem too rigid right now. I need a place where I can share all that is going on in my life. Can we try a less structured approach where you do more listening?
- Our sessions seem too directionless. I'm not making the connection between what we're doing and how

it's supposed to help me. Can we discuss how to add more structure in my treatment plan?

Meta-Communication

Meta-communication is the ability to talk about how well you're communicating. During a counseling session, be more aware of how well you're connecting and communicating. Here are some examples of what you might say:
- I've been talking the whole session. Am I talking too much?
- I didn't say that very well. Do you understand what I'm trying to say? Can you summarize what you've heard so far?
- How am I coming across to you? What are you feeling while I'm talking?
- You seem like you don't want to hurt my feelings. I give you permission to speak your mind.
- I didn't understand the last couple of sentences. Can you say it again in a different way?
- I don't like it when your voice gets that loud. If you'll speak softer, it will help me to stay in the conversation.

Immediacy

Immediacy is the ability to share with someone how you're feeling in real time. Just because your response is negative, doesn't mean anyone has done anything wrong. It only means that when 'A' happens, you feel 'B.' Practice sharing how you're feeling in the moment. Here are some examples:
- When you suggested I confront my husband, I felt anxious.

- When you challenge me to be my best self, I feel happy and empowered.
- When you're honest with me, even if you have bad news, I feel respected.
- When you interrupt me, I believe you care more about your agenda than you care about me. Then I feel unimportant.
- When you raise your voice like that, I feel like a cornered animal.
- I feel angry when you don't provide much feedback to me.
- I'm feeling shame now that I spilled my guts to you.

Putting Them Together

When you combine all three it might look something like this:
- I'm noticing that we seem to be talking around the issue. I feel uncomfortable for some reason. How do you feel?

Chapter 10

Build Therapeutic Trust

For counseling to work well, you need to be able to reveal your weaknesses. To feel safe enough to be vulnerable, you need to be able to trust your counselor.

Trust is an essential ingredient in any successful relationship. Many people seek counseling because someone has betrayed them. Feeling scared to trust will make counseling more challenging. If you have trust issues, consider making the initial focus of your counseling the strengthening of your ability to trust. As you explore trust in your personal life, see how trust (or distrust) shows up in your counseling relationship.

If you don't trust your counselor, you probably won't ask for help when you need it most. Then, how will your counselor be able to address the heart of your struggle? When the counseling relationship is working well, you can share the areas where you feel the most shame. Experiencing acceptance where you feel most broken is how deep healing takes place.

Counseling works best when you can drop your guard and be vulnerable. Positive results are more likely when you:
- Understand and believe in the counseling process.
- Disclose your true self.
- Practice your counselor's suggestions.
- Resolve any conflict with your counselor (the next chapter will cover this in more detail).
- Embrace the necessary changes to reach your goals.

Trust Perceptively

Healthy trust is being vulnerable with others to the degree they have been trustworthy. To trust perceptively:
- Be initially open to relationship by testing another's trustworthiness.
- Adjust your boundaries depending on the safety of the environment (the safer the people and environment, the more vulnerable you can be).
- Seek mutual agreement whenever possible but be comfortable with disagreement.
- Be aware that only heaven is totally safe and only God is totally trustworthy.
- Avoid black and white thinking; no one is all good or all bad.
- Trust others' words and actions — for a trustworthy person these will line up. Maybe a person is trustworthy, but you don't feel like trusting. This might be an opportunity to grow your ability to trust. Maybe a person isn't acting trustworthy, but you want to trust them anyway. This might be the best time to wait patiently so you aren't unnecessarily hurt.

Help Me Help You

Trust Building

If you want to build trust you must be trustworthy and also be prepared to risk. To build trust:

- If you are confused or puzzled about a person's behavior, seek clarification. To avoid misunderstanding, ask them why they made a particular statement.
- Don't assume you understand another's motivations.
- Tell others when you feel unable to trust.
- Look and see the positive. Give each new person a chance; recognize and avoid making unilateral vows ("all men are untrustworthy").
- Be willing to work through conflict when it arises.
- Be consistent with who you are. Don't make sudden moves away or toward others.
- Find the balancing point between your optimal time together and time apart.
- Have courage to take educated risks to be more transparent. Share your concerns, dreams, hopes, fears, doubts, successes, and failures.
- Be transparent with who you are even when it means exposing your differences and highlighting disagreements.
- Don't expect you will never get hurt or will never be disappointed.

Spiritual Trust Myths

The God you are afraid to trust isn't the true Living God, instead, He is the false god you've created. False beliefs about God set you up for feeling betrayed by God. The following might seem like they are true, but they are actually false:

- God will never let anything bad happen to me (John 16:33).
- Life is fair.
- Conflict always means someone is wrong or has sinful behavior.
- Christians should always feel peace.
- God will fix any problem I have according to my expectations.
- God doesn't really care about me.
- If I am obedient I can avoid pain and problems.
- If I am obedient God will give me what I want.

Do you see yourself in any of these? What problems do such false beliefs create? How would you change these statements so they are true? Will you come to God, asking that He help you to unconditionally trust Him and perceptively trust others?

Chapter 11

Resolve Conflict

No one likes conflict, but the skill of resolving conflict will serve you well and help you reach your life goals. Most conflict involving intense, negative emotions is a result of misunderstandings and perceived hurts. Thorough communication can clear up most issues.

What better place is there to resolve conflict than in counseling with your counselor who wants to help you succeed? If you feel offended or hurt by your counselor, that's a perfect opportunity to use your counseling relationship to practice resolving conflict.

Conflict Is Normal

Any relationship can naturally develop unresolved conflict, and the counseling relationship is no exception. Your counselor is a regular person like you, but has some additional training and experience. Your counselor isn't perfect, so you might need to occasionally work through your differences, disagreements, or disappointments.

The steps to resolve conflict are the same as with any relationship. Seek understanding first; don't problem solve until you understand each other. To improve understanding, describe your experience and use active listening. Each person has a reason for their particular behavior. Try to make that reason clear. After you understand each other, work out an agreeable solution. Because this will benefit you, conflict resolution should always take place during your sessions (not any other time).

Conflict Is Neutral

Conflict is only problematic when participants use it as a means to hurt one another. Otherwise, conflict is an opportunity to learn more about who you are and who others are. Conflict is merely an attempt to establish healthy boundaries. Once you know what you are willing to do or not willing to do, you can better negotiate a solution.

The more you know yourself, the easier it is to resolve conflict. For example, pretend you and a friend are deciding what kind of food to eat. If you know you have a strong dislike for seafood, you can clearly say so. Then all you have to decide is if you are still willing to go to a seafood restaurant. If so, you would need to determine the conditions of your willingness.

Conflict Is Complicated

An argument over a simple decision, like where to eat, that becomes over-heated must involve other complications. The energy that escalates the conflict doesn't come from the decision immediately before you. It comes from a broader sense of your wellbeing. You might insist on eating where you like the food for several reasons. Maybe when you were a child your parents always took you to a restaurant where you hated the food. Or, the last time you ate at a particular restaurant, you got sick.

The same negative impressions that can happen with food can also happen in relationships. If your dad was abusive to you as a child, you might believe that all men are going to hurt you. If you strongly mistrust a new male in your life, it most likely has little to do with the new person (someone you hardly know) but everything to do with an old relationship.

In counseling, when you confuse your counselor with someone from your life (whether in the past or present) and over-react as if your counselor was that person, it's called transference. It's a normal part of relationships, so it's also normal to work through any conflict that results from it.

Could you be projecting experiences with other people onto your counselor? You could have a small issue with your counselor, but it feels big because it reminds you of other painful life events. If you can be aware of how this is happening, you can use it to your advantage during your time with your counselor. If you can resolve the issue with your counselor, it should be easier to resolve the other more challenging events.

Counter-transference occurs when your counselor confuses you with someone from their life. It can be equally important to identify when this happens. However, since this is more about your counselor, it should only be discussed in your counseling to the degree that talking about it helps you. Otherwise, your counselor should deal with their issues on their own time. Counselors often participate in their own counseling.

Conflict, along with a willingness to resolve it, is a way to grow rather than a reason to not trust your counselor or quit counseling. Speaking about your feelings, including what is bothering you, is often necessary to begin the resolution process. If counseling isn't going well, simply talking about any unspoken conflict or tension can make a huge difference.

Chapter 12

Continue Until You Reach Your Goals

There isn't a specific time limit for counseling. So how long should you attend? Keep going as long as you are benefiting from it.

Counseling will generally last longer the more challenging your goals are. A challenging goal might not always be easy or fun to achieve. So, it's important to know the best and worst reasons to stop counseling.

The worst time to end counseling is if you will miss out on a growth opportunity in a supportive environment. Just because you feel uncomfortable doesn't mean you should quit counseling. You came to counseling because something was uncomfortable in your life, right? So, if possible, stay the course until you reach your goals.

There are three main scenarios when it makes sense for you to terminate counseling:

1. You have achieved your goals.

2. You have run out of resources.
3. Your counseling is consistently unproductive.

Achieved Goals

The optimal way to end counseling is when you have fulfilled the reasons you are seeking counseling. Goals are extremely important. If you don't know what your goals are, how will you be able to determine if you've reached them? The best way to end counseling is by mutual agreement that counseling has served its purpose for you at this time in your life. Even if you've reached your initial goal, you might now realize you have other goals that are important to you. It's okay to continue counseling with a different goal than the one you originally brought to counseling.

Lack Resources

If you haven't completed your goals, but you honestly lack an important resource (such as time, money, or appropriate motivation), you might be better off ending counseling until you are ready to make it a higher priority. But before you do, reconsider your goals. Have they changed? Maybe you'll realize your goals are worth the continued investment. Is there something else that you can (temporarily) give up, to make room for your goals?

Lack Fit

Being confident in your counselor's ability to help you is important. Sometimes what a counselor can offer and what you need don't match up well. But before you give up, try to discern if there is something you are missing that would be a problem with any counselor.

First, have you attempted to create a customized treatment plan? Part of the work of counseling is to learn how to determine what your goals are. If you need a more detailed plan, tell your counselor you want help focusing on your goals.

If you can't reach agreement with your counselor on what is best for you (your goals and how to reach them), that could be a sign it's time to move on. Sometimes what you want or need isn't in the areas of your counselor's abilities or specialization.

Second, have you attempted to resolve any actual or perceived conflict? Part of the work of counseling is to learn how to resolve conflict with another person.

If you're not receiving what you need, try reviewing your goals and discussing your expectations for counseling. Your counselor might think everything is going well, unless you tell your counselor how your expectations aren't met. Counseling is challenging work. You could be experiencing frustration with the counseling process, not a lack of a good fit with your counselor.

If you've tried to find resolution and have reached an impasse, then it might be time to move on. An inexperienced counselor or a counselor who doesn't understand your needs could add more frustration instead of helping to reduce it.

Whether your therapy is going well and you've achieved your goals, or not so well and you need other help, tell your counselor you're ending therapy. Whenever possible, discuss ending therapy with your counselor in session. Whenever possible explain why. Have you reached your goals? Are you stuck and not making progress? If you part ways, your counselor can help you understand what to look for in your next counselor.

Afterword

Go and Grow

Counseling can be an amazing process of changing your perspective on life for the better. It works best when you openly share your hurt with your counselor, who is trained to help. When it's working, no other intervention can compare to the benefits you will receive. You can experience an increasing excitement to live.

Revisit and Revise Your Goals

Whether you are continuing to seek the help of your counselor or you are working on your own, reaching your goals is important. Keep your momentum going by evaluating your progress regularly. I suggest once a month.

How far have you come to reaching your goals? For each goal, keep track of its start date, percent complete, and anticipated or actual finish date. Maybe you're realizing that your original goals aren't what you really need to be focused on. If so, don't worry. This is a sign that counseling is working. You're becoming more aware of what you need.

Review the Goal Setting form you filled out earlier. If your goals have changed, fill out a new form. If not, make necessary changes to bring your goals up to date with what you know today. Use the following questions to evaluate your progress, then share your findings with your counselor.

Questions to Help You Revise Your Goals

- What is the most significant thing you've wanted to accomplish but haven't yet?
- What is the most significant thing you've learned about yourself?
- What have you gained from your counseling that you wish you knew a year ago?
- Are you discovering any new goals you want to work on?
- Where do you want to be in a year from now?

Counseling is an awesome process for finding a positive way forward. I wish you an increasing amount of freedom as you pursue your own personal growth.

Do you have a question or an experience to share? Would you like to share how has this book been a blessing to you? Contact me at mpavlik@christianconcepts.com.

ABOUT MATT PAVLIK

Matt Pavlik is a licensed professional clinical counselor who wants each individual restored to their true identity. He completed his Masters in Clinical Pastoral Counseling from Ashland Theological Seminary and his Bachelors in Computer Science from the University of Illinois.

He's been a Christian since 1991 and started journaling around that time. Matt and his wife Georgette have been married since 1999 and live with their four children in Centerville, Ohio.

Blogger

Learn more at ChristianConcepts. com.

Professional Counselor

Matt has more than 15 years of experience counseling individuals and couples at his Christian private practice, New Reflections Counseling (NewReflectionsCounseling.com).

Author

Matt's books help you grow into the person you were made to be. See detailed information at http://christianconcepts.com/books.

Identity Books

To Identity and Beyond demonstrates that the only path to enjoying your life is the journey from where you are at to your place in heaven.

Confident Identity shows you what your identity is and isn't through detailed exercises that culminate in you writing your identity portrait.

Marriage Book

Marriage From Roots To Fruits is a comprehensive workbook with 50 lessons to teach you the techniques to maintain a healthy relationship.

Journaling Books

Soar Like Eagles introduces you to the journal-in-layers method designed to help you journal for emotional growth.

Each *Journal Your Way* book focuses on a core longing (hope, significance, or love) to apply the journal-in-layers method to your devotional life. Each lesson provides scriptures, a quote, a picture, and encouraging reflections to jumpstart your heart. You'll be surprised what insights you gain when you review the thoughts and feelings you wrote in your journal.